# Online Multi-Level Marketing Mastery
## *Building Your Network and Profits*

# Table of Contents

# Chapter 1. Introduction

Introducing our Special Report: "Online Multi-Level Marketing Mastery: Building Your Network and Profits"! This Special Report is the golden ticket for those ambitious individuals, ready to dive headfirst into the dynamic and highly rewarding universe of online multi-level marketing. Handcrafted by a team of experts, this report not only unveils the secrets to building a successful network but also serves as your guide to staggering profits. It sweeps across a range of topics, from the fundamentals of multi-level marketing, to the art of recruiting and retaining members, to tactical profit-increasing strategies. Even if you're stepping onto the first rung of the MLM ladder or you're an experienced marketer, this report is guaranteed to catapult your journey to heights you've only dreamt of. Ready to change your life? Get your hands on this report and ignite your future in MLM with a bang!

# Chapter 2. Understanding Multi-Level Marketing: Online Platforms and Their Potential

The online arena for Multi-Level Marketing (MLM) serves as a conducive environment to foster growth and unlock immense business potential. Harnessing this potential, however, rests on your understanding of what MLM truly entails and how to make online platforms work to your advantage.

## 2.1. MLM is More Than a Business Model

Fundamentally, MLM is a business model that incentivizes distributors to recruit new members into their network. It's a tiered system where rewards are earned through personal sales and the sales of those recruited into the distributor's network. MLM allows distributors to work from the comfort of their homes, reach a global audience and build a business that provides passive income.

Beyond this fundamental structure, MLM is an opportunity to build personal and financial independence. It gives individuals the chance to hone their leadership skills, broaden their social connections, and learn the nitty-gritty of running a business. Furthermore, MLM enables anyone with entrepreneurial spirit and a determination to succeed an opportunity to enter the world of business without requiring extensive capital.

## 2.2. The Online Advantage

In today's technologically advanced world, MLM has been revolutionized by online platforms. The internet not only allows for broader outreach, but also brings in a level of convenience and scalability previously unmatched. Conducting MLM activities online paves the way for a faster and more efficient recruitment process. Virtual meetings, online presentations and webinars deliver your message effectively without the constraints of physical boundaries.

Additionally, the integration of social media platforms with MLM strategies has opened up doors to a vast audience. You can use these platforms to reach people with shared interests, promote your products, share testimonials and engage directly with prospective recruits.

## 2.3. Maneuvering Through Various Online Platforms

Different online platforms offer unique advantages for MLM.

- Websites: An attractive, user-friendly website can serve as the home base for your MLM business. It's a platform where people can learn more about your products and business opportunity, and contact you for details or sign up.

- Social Media: Networks like Facebook, Instagram, LinkedIn and Twitter are excellent platforms for reaching out to potential recruits and customers. These platforms can be used for brand promotion, customer engagement, sharing success stories and more.

- Blogs: Blogs allow for the sharing of detailed information about your MLM business and products. They can be utilized to provide educational content, industry news, and even motivational stories to inspire others to join your network.

- Videos: Platforms like YouTube are perfect for showcasing your products and the value of your MLM opportunity. Videos allow for a more engaging and interactive experience, helping to build trust and establish credibility.

Beyond selecting the appropriate platforms, you need to learn how to optimally use them. Understand the functionalities, audiences and trends of each platform. Tailor your content and strategies accordingly to yield maximum results.

# 2.4. Leveraging the Potential of Online MLM

The dynamism and flexibility of online platforms for MLM pose numerous benefits. These benefits, however, can be fully realized only when the potential of online MLM is leveraged correctly. A few strategies to accomplish this are:

1. Utilize digital tools: Digital tools can significantly improve your MLM performance. Customer Relationship Management tools, email marketing software, and social media scheduling tools can streamline your MLM activities while ensuring maximum reach and impact.

2. Develop a substantial online presence: Visibility is key in the online arena. Build your identity through consistent and authentic communication. Regularly update your social media profiles and websites with content that resonates with your audience.

3. Leverage SEO: Search Engine Optimization helps to increase your online visibility. Incorporate SEO strategies in your web content and blogs to rank higher on search results, thus improving your chances of attracting potential recruits and customers.

4. Build and manage your online community: Establishing an online community means creating a space for your audience to interact,

engage and grow. Regularly interacting with your community, asking for their opinions, and addressing their concerns helps in building trust and loyalty.

5. Stay updated: The online world is ever-changing. Stay updated with the latest trends and techniques and incorporate them into your online MLM strategy to ensure continued success.

In conclusion, understanding the nuances of MLM and the potential of online platforms is crucial to achieving success in the MLM industry. By leveraging the opportunities that online platforms present, you can build a profitable MLM business that is not only sustainable but also adaptable to the changing landscape of the digital world.

# Chapter 3. Deciphering the MLM Business Model: A Comprehensive Breakdown

Before embarking on the journey of Multi-Level Marketing (MLM), it is paramount to understand its business model thoroughly. Rooted in direct selling methodologies, MLM is a complex but rewarding architecture that emphasizes the duality of selling products and recruiting members to the network.

## 3.1. The Multi-Level Nature

The name 'multi-level marketing' emanates from its structural design. In traditional direct selling, individuals referred to as distributors, consultants, or associates, are recruited by a company to sell its products or services directly to consumers. MLM brings an added layer to this concept - promoting distributors to recruit a downline of distributors. Therefore, in MLM, you make money not only through direct sales but also from the sales made by the people you've introduced into the business, creating a hierarchical commission-based system. This motif of multiple levels of distributors, all actively promoting and selling, characterizes the true essence of the MLM business model.

Here's an example to illustrate the multi-level aspect:

In the above MLM hierarchy, 'A' is at the top level who directly recruited 'B' and 'C'. Now, 'A' earns commissions not just from personal sales, but from the sales made by B and C as well. The story doesn't end here. If 'C' recruits 'D' and 'E', 'A' is again entitled to a share from 'D' and 'E's sales too, thereby engendering multiple levels of compensation.

## 3.2. MLM vs Pyramid Schemes

While MLM's design is seemingly similar to that of pyramid schemes, understanding the differences between the two is vital as confusing them can lead to severe legal issues. Pyramid schemes are illegal and focus primarily on recruitment rather than selling a viable product or service. On the other hand, MLM is legitimate and product-focused. In MLM, the real money is from product sales, and recruitment is just part of the strategy to increase product sales.

## 3.3. Products and Services

Products and services are the lifeblood of MLM companies. They could range from physical products such as cosmetics, nutrition supplements, or household goods to services like internet marketing tools or health and wellness services. The quality and usability of these products or services are key factors in an MLM's success, influencing not only customer satisfaction but also distributor retention.

## 3.4. Recruitment: The Second Tier of Profit

Recruiting is the second aspect of the MLM business model. Distributors are incentivized to recruit more people into the business. These new recruits, referred to as a distributor's 'downline', provide another source of income. The more people a distributor recruits, the higher the distributor moves in the hierarchy, and the larger their potential to earn from the downline's sales.

## 3.5. Compensation Plan

The compensation structure or plan is a complex element of MLM that can vary significantly. Usually, MLM companies have a multi-tiered compensation plan where the earnings increase as a distributor moves up levels. This is the ultimate driver for distributors to not only sell but also expand their downlines. There are several types of compensation plans within the industry, the most popular being Binary, Unilevel, and Matrix plans, each having its unique distribution of sales and recruitment commissions.

## 3.6. The Pros and Cons of MLM

Like any other business model, MLM too has its advantages and drawbacks. Some of the positives include low start-up costs, the flexibility of working hours, personal growth, and the potential for high returns. Conversely, the downsides encompass the possibility of low initial earning rates, the demand for regular networking and recruiting, and a negative reputation stemming mostly from pyramid scheme confusion or failed MLM businesses.

## 3.7. MLM Legalities

MLM is legal, provided it adheres to certain regulations such as focusing on product sales and not solely recruiting, being transparent about the compensation plan, and maintaining honest marketing practices. Distributors should make sure the MLM company they choose is abiding by these rules to stay clear of potential legal trouble and ensure a lawful operation.

Unpacking the MLM business model might seem like a daunting task, but it's a solid foundation for setting your path in the industry. Knowledge of the essential elements, understanding the key differentiators, and legalities, and being wary of the potential pitfalls arm you with the arsenal needed to succeed in this vibrant, profit-filled world. The more well-versed you are in the model, the more prepared you'll be to navigate the MLM seas—a journey filled with challenges, but also ripe with rewards.

# Chapter 4. The Power of Recruitment: Strategies and Techniques

Recruitment stands as the pillar of a successful Multi-Level Marketing (MLM). The strength, dedication, and commitment of your network undeniably dictate the trajectory of your MLM journey. This chapter aims to equip you with a range of strategies and tactics that will aid you in attracting and onboarding potential members to your network.

## 4.1. Understanding Your Product And its Market

The inaugural step in the recruitment process begins much before you actually start approaching potential recruits; it starts with your understanding of the product and its market. You cannot hope to convince others to be a part of your marketing network if you, yourself, are not confident in the product's value. Equip yourself with comprehensive knowledge about your product, its unique selling points (USPs), its market, and potential customers.

Once this foundation is established, it becomes much easier to recruit potential members. You can present them with a clear vision and expose them to the opportunities your product can open for them.

## 4.2. Identifying the Ideal Candidate

Not everyone can be (or should be) recruited for your MLM network. Adopting a 'mass recruitment' strategy will only lead to inefficiency and unmanageable teams. It's crucial to identify the ideal candidate who will contribute positively to your network. This typically includes individuals who are ambitious, driven, independent, and have a flair for sales and marketing.

The identification of an ideal candidate not only improves your network's efficiency, it also aids in maintaining a low attrition rate by ensuring that the recruited members have a genuine interest and capability in carrying out the tasks required in MLM marketing.

# 4.3. Communication: The Key to Successful Recruitment

Communication plays a pivotal role in the recruitment strategy. It encapsulates conveying the right message to the potential candidate, understanding their needs and concerns, handling their objections, and ultimately, ensuring a seamless transfer of information.

Your recruit's first impression of the MLM opportunity lies in how you communicate with them. Display optimism, enthusiasm, and sincerity. Demonstrate the potential of the MLM network and how it can play a role in their lives. Remember, the art of recruitment lies in selling the opportunity more than the product.

# 4.4. Building Trust with Potential Recruits

In this era of scams and fraudulent schemes, trust plays an even more profound role than it did before. Prospective members would only want to be part of your MLM network if they can trust you. You need to assure them about the legitimacy of your network. Talk about your achievements and share testimonies from your existing members.

Remember, trust cannot be built in a day. It needs to be established over time through consistent and open communication, displaying genuine concern for your recruits' success, and fulfilling all promises.

# 4.5. Tailor Your Message to Your Recruit

Understand that each individual is unique; what might work for one recruit might not work for another. It's essential to adapt your recruiting pitch to suit each potential recruit. Determine what they need and shape your message to explain precisely how your MLM business can fill those gaps.

# 4.6. Conclusion: Recruitment as an Ongoing Process

Recruitment shouldn't be viewed as a one-time task; instead, it is a continuous process. A successful MLM marketer is perpetually recruiting – not just to continually expand but also to replace members in the network who may inevitably leave. It's about gaining the right momentum and maintaining an ongoing recruitment drive. A comprehensive recruitment strategy should be geared towards consistent recruitment, maintaining your team's quality, and focusing on team members' growth and success. By mastering recruitment, your MLM business can soar to unprecedented heights.

In conclusion, the recruitment journey in MLM marketing is a challenging persuasion exercise that requires clarity, effort, trust, and, most importantly, persistence. By practicing these techniques and strategies, you are bound to witness a significant improvement in your network's reach, effectiveness, and profitability.

# Chapter 5. Building and Nurtifying Your Downline: Creating a Thriving Network

Building and nurturing your downline is at the heart of multi-level marketing. This process can be broken down into five steps: recruitment, effective communication, providing support, leadership development, and active retention. Through strategic implementation of these steps, you can create a thriving, profitable network.

## 5.1. Recruitment: Finding the Right Individuals

The first step in constructing your downline is finding potential team members. Start by identifying your target demographic and devising a recruitment strategy that appeals directly to them. This includes understanding where they spend their time, their interests, and, most importantly, their needs, and how your MLM can fulfill them.

Social networks are a powerful tool for recruitment, providing direct access to prospective team members. Share engaging content that highlights the benefits of joining your network, showing them how it can improve their lives. Live videos, infographics, personal testimonials, and business tutorials can be particularly effective at capturing interest.

Remember that it's not just about the number of people you recruit, but the quality. You want individuals who are committed, eager to learn, and ready to invest their time and effort. To identify them, consider factors like their working history, commitment to personal growth, and entrepreneurial spirit.

## 5.2. Effective communication: The Key to Connection

Once you have recruits, maintaining an open line of communication is essential. Regularly reaching out can help show them they're part of a supportive, dedicated community. Regular updates keep everyone in the loop while personalized messages can help foster a stronger connection.

Good communication practices include prompt responses, clear and concise explanations, and regular feedback. Encourage open dialogue, allowing your team members to voice their ideas, concerns, and aspirations. Also, promote a positive environment, acknowledging successes and introducing constructive solutions to problems.

## 5.3. Providing Support: A Pillar of Success

Support comes in many forms: training, mentorship, resources, or simply a helping hand. When team members feel supported, they're more likely to invest their time and effort, which drives the growth of your network.

New recruits may require extensive training about the products, the business strategy, or MLM practices. Make this process as comprehensive and straightforward as possible, ensuring they can put their knowledge to use immediately.

Mentorship provides a more personalized approach to support. Give your downline regular access to you or experienced team members who can guide them through hurdles and inspire them to reach their potential.

Offer plenty of resources – guides, tutorials, tools – that can assist your team members to excel.

## 5.4. Leadership Development: Cultivating Future Leaders

Your downline must also learn to become leaders, able to guide their own recruits (your "second-level" downline). By cultivating leadership skills within your group, you're preparing your downline for success and longevity.

Identify individuals who possess the potential to lead and develop that potential. This may entail additional training, granting them more responsibilities, or providing them with unique opportunities to shine. Make sure they understand the importance of their role and provide them with the tools to excel as leaders.

## 5.5. Active Retention: Keeping Your Network Intact

Recruiting a downline isn't a one-and-done deal; you must also retain your team members. Retention involves regular check-ins, showing appreciation, providing ongoing support and training, and identifying any potential issues early on.

When team members feel acknowledged and valued for their contributions, they're more likely to stick with your network. Recognize milestones and exceptional work, whether with a simple thank-you message or a small incentive.

Offer support, especially during rough patches. If a team member struggles, step in and assist, helping them overcome the challenges and come out stronger. It's these moments that build trust and loyalty, reinforcing your network's solidity.

Remember, building and nurturing your downline is a journey, not an overnight feat. And with patience, perseverance, and strategic implementation of these steps, you'll create not just a downline, but a thriving community of dedicated team members, ready to propel your MLM business to unprecedented heights.

# Chapter 6. The Science of Retention: Keeping Your Network Active and Growing

In the world of online multi-level marketing, the success of your business stands on the foundation of an active and growing network. Using scientific principles, we can maximize the retention of your team and, by extension, the profitability of your enterprise.

## 6.1. Understanding Retention

Understanding retention in the context of multi-level marketing is much more than just having members who stick around. It involves nurturing the relationships you have, creating meaningful engagement among members and providing them with opportunities and incentives to maintain their active participation. Knowing the factors that determine whether someone will stay or leave is crucial in ensuring the growth and activity of your network.

### 6.1.1. The Importance of Connection

Engendering a feeling of 'belonging' is essential for retention. When members feel a sense of community and a personal connection with the team, they are more likely to remain active. This involves active communication and collaboration among members, the encouragement of shared goals and values, and ensuring each member feels valued and understood.

# 6.2. Creating a Strong Support System

Every successful organization has a robust support system that not only helps new members get acclimated but also aids in the continued growth and development of existing members. This support system should provide a safe space for members to express their concerns and challenges and offer tools to help them confront and overcome these challenges.

### 6.2.1. Effective Communication Channels

In the digital age, effective communication goes beyond the traditional phone calls and emails. Now, MLM businesses leverage social media platforms, instant messaging, webinars, and other digital platforms for team communication. Quick and open communication is also crucial in addressing any potential issues before they escalate.

### 6.2.2. Continuous Learning Opportunities

Providing opportunities for learning and development shows your commitment to your team members' success and encourages them to stay. This can be in the form of regular training sessions on new marketing strategies, business development courses, or motivational talks.

# 6.3. The Power of Recognition and Incentive Structures

Recognition and incentives are powerful tools in the toolbox of retention. These provide tangible demonstrations of the value and importance members have in your MLM business.

### 6.3.1. Invest in Recognition Systems

Acknowledging your team members' hard work promotes a sense of achievement. Regularly celebrate their milestones and successes, no matter how small they may seem. This boosts their morale and gives them additional motivation to remain part of your network.

### 6.3.2. Develop Incentive Structures

An effective incentive structure can attract and retain members. Whether these incentives come in the form of goods, cash rewards, discounts, or exclusive opportunities, it can motivate members to engage more actively and contribute significantly towards network growth.

# 6.4. Implementing Effective Follow-Up Strategies

Follow-ups are vital for maintaining engagement and ensuring that members don't feel left behind or forgotten.

### 6.4.1. Regular Check-ins

Regularly checking in with your team members helps you keep track of their progress and offer the necessary support they may require. These check-ins can also provide the opportunity to offer feedback and advice, keeping your members engaged and motivated.

### 6.4.2. Consistent Feedback Loops

Encouraging continuous feedback helps to create a culture of open communication. It allows you to spot any potential issues early and resolve them before they become bigger problems.

In conclusion, retention in multi-level marketing is a science that involves understanding human connection, creating strong support systems, recognition, incentive structures, and effective follow-up strategies. By mastering these elements, you can keep your network active, thriving and set yourself up for long-term MLM success.

# Chapter 7. Maximizing Profits: Shifting Your Revenue into Overdrive

In the ever-evolving universe of online multi-level marketing (MLM), maximizing profits goes beyond merely growing your network. It involves strategizing and shrewd decision-making to optimize your revenue stream. Let's delve into how you can steer your income into overdrive.

## 7.1. Understanding Your Revenue Streams

Primarily, MLM offers two major revenue streams: direct sales and team sales. Direct sales are the commissions you earn from selling the products or services to consumers directly, while team sales are the bonuses earned from the sales made by your network. Mastering the art of maximizing these two streams will boost your earnings significantly.

All MLM companies structure their compensation plans differently. Take time to understand your company's compensation plan inside out, understanding the performance metrics, qualification criteria for sales bonuses, incentives, and whether any opportunities might be left untapped. Remember, in MLM, knowledge is the cornerstone of maximizing performance.

## 7.2. The Art of Upselling and Cross-selling

Upselling and cross-selling are great strategies to amplify your direct sales. Upselling involves persuading your customer to purchase additional items or more expensive items for perceived added value. On the other hand, cross-selling encourages the purchase of a complementary product.

The key is to listen to your customers' preferences and needs, then determine how adding to their purchase can enhance the value gained. By doing so, not only are you maximizing your revenue, but also improving customer satisfaction, thereby creating a win-win situation.

## 7.3. Focus on Customer Retention

In MLM, it's much easier and cost-effective to sell to existing customers than it is to venture out and acquire new ones. Your existing customer base is your gold mine. They trust you, engage with your product or services, and establish a recurring revenue stream.

Implement customer retention strategies by touching base regularly, keeping them updated with new products or services, and providing customer appreciation incentives. Work on offering personal touches for your customers, such as sending birthday notes, creating personalized offers, or simplifying the delivery process. Retaining a loyal customer base guarantees steady revenue and, in turn, maximizes profits.

## 7.4. Build and Educate Your Team

In the MLM world, your progress is not solely determined by your efforts. Your team forms the backbone of your success. Therefore, substantial time and resources should be dedicated to building a capable and dedicated team.

It's not enough to recruit team members; nurturing and educating them is paramount. Provide ongoing training on product knowledge, sales techniques, and marketing strategies. Aim to create confident ambassadors for your products or services. When your team succeeds, you succeed.

## 7.5. Fine-Tune Your Marketing Skills

MLM, at its core, is sales and marketing. Fine-tuning your marketing skills can significantly increase your customer base and, by extension, your profits. Use of traditional marketing techniques, like warm marketing and referrals, combined with digital marketing avenues, such as email marketing, content marketing, and social media marketing, can dramatically expand your reach.

Marketing strategies change with evolving consumer behaviors and market trends, so continuous learning and adaptability are crucial. Your commitment is your currency in boosting sales and profits.

## 7.6. Planning for Long-Term Success

In MLM, success is not an overnight phenomenon. It demands strategic planning, sustained effort, and patience. Developing plans for your long-term success involves setting realistic goals, monitoring your progress regularly, learning from your failures, and celebrating your successes.

More than the numbers, long-term success relies on building strong relationships in your network and customer base, as well as improving your personal and your team's skills.

Remember, the journey to shifting your revenue into overdrive in MLM is a marathon, not a sprint. Treat it as a business, be patient, stay dedicated, and the path to financial success will be open to you.

# Chapter 8. Online Presence: Branding and Audience Engagement Techniques

It comes as no surprise that a robust online presence today means the difference between obscurity and popularity, between stagnation and success. As you embark on your pursuit of mastering online multi-level marketing (MLM), incorporating online branding and audience engagement techniques is critical. Unlike physical MLM, the online arena is highly dynamic and competitive. Here, you are not just your products or services, you are a brand, a beacon of trust and value that people want to be associated with.

## 8.1. Building Your Personal Brand

Your personal brand is, in essence, a promise to your clients. It communicates what they can expect from you and, more importantly, differentiates your products from your competitors. It's derived from who you are, who you want to be, and who people perceive you to be. A robust personal brand bridges the gap of anonymity and lends credibility to your online MLM business.

1. Discover your Brand Identity: Understand your strengths, areas of expertise, unique selling propositions, and the market needs you are committed to serving.

2. Align Personal and Business Values: Your personal values should be in alignment with your business values as it establishes credibility and trust.

3. Develop a Personal Brand Statement: This should vividly summarize your brand's key aspects in a concise, compelling way. It sets the tone for all your subsequent interactions and communications.

4. Consistent Branding across Channels: Adapt your brand and brand statement to fit across various online platforms, like your website, social media, and email marketing campaigns.

## 8.2. Enhancing Your Web Presence

If your brand is the face of your online MLM, your website is its physical shape. It should engage and educate prospects while facilitating interactions and business transactions.

1. Aesthetic and Responsive Design: The first rule is to make your website visually appealing and easy to navigate. Simplicity, clarity, and quick load times are key, along with compatibility with mobile devices.

2. Value-driven Content: The content should centre on your brand's strong points. Highlight your unique selling points, benefits provided, and customer success stories to attract and retain prospects.

3. SEO Practices: Implementing SEO (Search Engine Optimization) practices makes your website more visible on search engines, bringing in more organic traffic.

4. Regular Blog Posts: A blog can cover related topics and provide valuable information to readers, aiding in credible branding while improving SEO.

## 8.3. Dominating Social Media

In the digital world, social media serves as your brand's voice. It offers a platform to directly engage with your audience, strengthening your brand's human aspect.

1. Select the Right Platforms: Focus on platforms where your target audience spends the most time. Each platform has its own nuances, understand them and tailor your strategy for each.

2. Create Valuable Content: Create content that resonates with your audience. Use attractive visuals, videos, infographics, or user-generated content to increase engagement.

3. Be Active: Stay engaged with your network. Respond to queries, comments, and take candid feedback. Be consistent with posts and interactions.

4. Monitor and Adapt: Constantly monitor your social media metrics to understand what works and what doesn't. Be flexible and willing to adapt your strategy based on these insights.

# 8.4. Providing Added Value

Your brand's offerings should consistently deliver added value to your audience, not solely in the form of products or services but also in terms of credible information.

1. Webinars/Podcasts: Host webinars or podcasts about your industry vertical. This positions you as a thought leader, builds credibility, and fosters a dedicated audience base.

2. E-books/Reports: Develop detailed e-books or reports on industry trends, forecasts, etc. Provide these for free to your audience in exchange for their contact information.

3. Value-added Emails: Send insightful, value-packed emails regularly to your audience. These should go beyond merely promoting your products but also educate, inspire, and engage.

4. Loyalty Programs: Establish loyalty programs for your audience. Offering benefits and rewards to loyal customers strengthens your relationship.

In conclusion, these branding and audience engagement techniques can rocket your online MLM business to new horizons. Building a powerful online presence is the lion's share of the work; couple it with a robust MLM system and unwavering determination, your success is guaranteed.

# Chapter 9. Overcoming Roadblocks: Handling Common MLM Challenges

Just as every rewarding journey, your venture into online multi-level marketing (MLM) will not be without obstacles. Learning them and incorporating strategic ways to mitigate them will greatly improve your chances at success. This chapter therefore pulls back the curtain on key challenges and how to effectively navigate them.

## 9.1. Understanding Common MLM Challenges

Before diving into specific strategies, it's important to recognize and understand the most common challenges that MLM professionals often encounter.

1. **Recruitment Difficulties:** This is one of the biggest challenges in MLM. Building a strong and motivated team is crucial for your success.

2. **Retention issues:** Efficacious recruiting isn't adequate, retaining team members is equally important. People leaving as fast as they join will hinder your growth.

3. **Lack of Training:** Many MLM professionals don't have adequate training in sales, marketing, and networking. This can lead to common errors and stunted growth.

4. **Misunderstanding the Business Model:** MLM has distinctive features that set it apart from traditional businesses. Inadequate understanding can lead to disillusionment and eventual failure.

5. **Market Saturation:** Many MLM products are in competitive

markets, making recruitment and sales difficult.

6. **Regulatory and Legal Issues:** MLMs must comply with laws that can vary from region to region. Ignorance of these can incur large penalties.

# 9.2. Overcoming Recruitment Difficulties

One of the fundamental aspects of MLM is recruitment. However, convincing people to join your network can be a daunting task. Here are key strategies to help you surmount this hurdle:

1. **Prospect continuously:** Regularly update your list of prospects and constantly reach out to them. Stay open to any potential lead.

2. **Devise a strategic recruitment plan:** Establish short-term and long-term recruitment goals. Tailor your approach to fit the target.

3. **Leverage your unique selling point (USP):** Define what makes your MLM opportunity unique and emphasize it during your pitch.

4. **Provide value:** Show potential recruits how joining your network will bring them value, be it financial, personal growth or networking opportunities.

# 9.3. Retention Strategies

Ensuring that members stay engaged and active in your network is a major challenge in MLM. The following strategies can help reinforce your retention efforts:

1. **Give Regular Training:** Regular and comprehensive training will give your team the confidence and skills to thrive.

2. **Foster a Supportive Culture:** By encouring collaboration and camaraderie, you bolster engagement and motivation.

3. **Provide Regular Feedback:** Regular, constructive feedback will assure your team members that they are valued.

4. **Offer Incentives:** Use incentives to spur motivation, these could take the form of bonuses, awards, or recognition.

# 9.4. Educating Your Team

Education is a vital component of any successful MLM professional's arsenal.

1. **Create useful educational material:** This might include video demonstrations, webinars, eBooks, or guides.

2. **Promote learning culture:** Encourage continuous learning by endorsing podcasts, seminars, or books related to MLM.

3. **Give demonstrations:** Show your team effective ways to pitch products, and recruit prospects. "Show, don't simply tell."

# 9.5. Dealing with Market Saturation

Market saturation is another common challenge in MLM. However, you can still attract prospects and make sales by:

1. **Focusing on a niche market:** By targeting a specific group, you can delineate yourself from the rest and attract a loyal consumer base.

2. **Emphasizing your product's unique qualities:** Distinguish your products from others by emphasizing their uniqueness and superiority.

3. **Adjusting your sales strategy:** Try a fresh approach to your sales and marketing approach to better fit the current market condition.

# 9.6. Managing Regulatory and Legal Issues

To avoid legal issues, MLM professionals must understand and adhere to the legalities governing their business.

1. **Stay informed:** Regularly update your knowledge of the rules and regulations in the MLM industry.

2. **Compliance training:** Make sure your network receives proper compliance training to prevent inadvertent legal breaches.

Facing challenges is part and parcel of the journey to MLM success. Overcoming these roadblocks will require creativity, resilience, strategy, and fortitude. However, by incorporating these tactics, you'll be well-equipped to create a thriving MLM business.

# Chapter 10. Compliance and Ethics: Setting the Standards for Business Practices

From the earliest stages of launching your multi-level marketing (MLM) journey, it's essential to practice and uphold the highest levels of compliance and ethics. Your commitment to a rock-solid ethical foundation will not only set the tone for your business practices but will also yield rewarding dividends—exponentially building trust within your ever-growing network of associates and clients.

## 10.1. Understanding Compliance in MLM

Compliance in MLM is essentially about adhering to the various rules, regulations, and laws that govern the MLM industry. These could be industry-specific rules, provincial or federal laws, or even international regulations—depending on the reach of your business.

The complexity of MLM compliance may sometimes feel daunting. However, consider this—a well-established compliance framework is like an insurance policy against legal threats and a reputation safety net for your business. It can assist in making informed decisions, minimizing legal risks, and fostering a transparent business environment.

1. **Federal and State Laws**: Understanding federal and state laws is fundamental to ensuring your MLM business operates within legal boundaries. For example, in the United States, the Federal Trade Commission (FTC) provides guidelines and regulations specifically for MLM companies. Awareness and compliance with these laws prevent legal mishaps and contribute to ethical

business practice.

2. **MLM Company Policies**: MLM companies typically have specific policies and regulations documented in their distributor policies and procedures. Distributors must follow these to ensure seamless operations. It includes details about distributor rights, company structure, compensation details, and more. Comprehending and adhering to these policies is crucial as it saves from potential pitfalls.

3. **International Regulations**: If your MLM business operates globally, you must become familiar with international regulations and laws pertaining to conducting MLM in those regions. The rules differ significantly from country to country, and a sound knowledge will help avoid inadvertent legal transgressions.

# 10.2. The Critical Role of Ethics in MLM

While compliance is about adhering to the rules, ethics is about making the right choices—even in the absence of rules. A holistic approach to ethics will ensure that your MLM business holds its ground on the principles of truthfulness, fairness, and respect.

1. **Transparency**: Being transparent with your network members about business practices, the potential return on investment, and any associated risks is the stepping stone to building trust. It is crucial that you avoid making exaggerated claims about potential income or the efficacy of products.

2. **Respect**: Respect for network members, employees, and customers is of utmost importance in running a successful MLM business. This includes respecting their time, efforts, and their commitments outside of the MLM ecosystem.

3. **Integrity**: A commitment to integrity implies abiding by the highest standards of business practice even in challenging

situations. It means standing by your word, fulfilling commitments, and making honest presentations.

# 10.3. Building a Compliance and Ethics Program

A compliance and ethics program incorporates training and monitoring activities into your day-to-day operations to ensure consistent adherence to both ethical standards and compliance requirements.

Start by creating a written code of conduct that outlines your company's commitment to compliance and ethical behavior. Distribute it to all members of your network and make sure they understand it completely. The code of conduct should be a guiding document that is occasionally revisited and updated as required.

The next step involves developing training programs that can inform and educate your network about their compliance responsibilities and importance of ethical behavior. The training can be conducted online and should be an ongoing process.

Implement monitoring systems to ensure that everyone adheres to the established compliance and ethics program. A third-party audit or regular internal reviews can help identify areas of non-compliance and provide opportunities to rectify them.

Lastly, encourage an open culture where employees or network members can report potential non-compliance without fear of retaliation. This openness can help the company identify and tackle issues before they escalate into significant problems.

# 10.4. The Golden Rule of MLM: People Over Profits

Understanding and practicing ethical conduct is paramount for the wave of success to flow through your MLM business. It warrants that all associates are treated fairly, their efforts are recognized, their achievements rewarded, and their problems addressed promptly and professionally. This should not be superseded by the urge to make quick profits. An MLM business built on the foundations of regulatory compliance and ethical standards, prepared to invest in its people's upliftment, can deliver sustained growth and success. Let's remember—our ethics and values are what define us, they are our business's lifeblood. Thus, make sure they represent the best of what you have to offer.

By setting and abiding by high standards, you ensure that your MLM business stands for integrity, respectfulness, and ethical best practices, embedding these principles in the heart of your network. Let these values be the driving forces of your MLM journey—all the way from the bottom to the top of the ladder. Your commitment to ethics and compliance will indeed serve as a beacon, guiding your business to shore, through the often tumultuous waters of multi-level marketing.

# Chapter 11. Sustaining Momentum: Long-Term Success in Online MLM

Profit sustainability in the multi-level marketing (MLM) industry makes for a daunting challenge. The ebb and flow nature of entrepreneurship, coupled with the pressures of a perpetually evolving online landscape can take a significant toll on maintaining momentum. Fortunately, with a strategic approach, a deep understanding of market trends, and an unwavering commitment to your network, it is wholly possible to not only persist but to prosper amidst the competition.

## 11.1. Cultivating MLM Success Mindset

As perceptive as it may sound, the journey towards long-term MLM success starts within. An entrepreneur with a success-oriented mindset approaches challenges as opportunities to learn rather than obstacles to overcome. Keeping a positive attitude aids in maintaining momentum and sustaining growth in the run of your MLM business.

- Stay Positive: The efficacy of a positive mindset should never be underestimated. Rejection and setbacks are part and parcel of any commercial endeavor. Those who view objections as opportunities for growth are more likely to bounce back from adversity than those who dwell on setbacks.

- Continuous Learning: Stay updated with the current trends, new tools, techniques, and strategies. Keeping yourself educated empowers you to adapt to changing online business environments.

- Fostering Tenacity: Persistence is a vital entrepreneurial trait. There will be highs and lows, but the key is to keep pushing. Remember, MLM rewards those who hang on and weather the storms of market fluctuation.

# 11.2. Setting Measurable Goals

Having clear and tangible goals in place is critical for sustaining momentum in MLM. Goals serve as beacons, guiding you through the cacophony of the online marketplace to the shores of success.

- Short-Term Goals: These are immediate objectives that provide a quick win and boost morale. They could range from signing up a certain number of new members to launching a brand-new online marketing campaign.

- Long-Term Goals: Long-term goals often serve as the 'big picture' - the ultimate success desired. It's critical to periodize them into manageable segments which, when accomplished in sequence, would lead to the attainment of the ultimate goal.

- Regular Review: Keep tracking progress against your goals. Adjust them as necessary and celebrate every accomplishment, no matter how small. This results in a positive feedback loop that fuels ongoing momentum.

# 11.3. Building a Strong Online Presence

In the digital realm, your presence signifies your brand. It's not just about having a website – it's about being discoverable, staying active, and engaging with your audience.

- Consistent Branding: Deploy consistent branding across all online platforms. This doesn't simply end at having a logo: it extends to the color scheme, tone and style of content, and overall customer experience.

- SEO Optimization: With sound SEO strategies, increase visibility in search engine results, thus driving increased organic traffic to your MLM network.

- Engage with Your Network: Consistently communicate and share valuable content with your network. This includes writing blog posts, running podcasts, webinars, or using email newsletters and social media posts.

# 11.4. Recruiting and Retaining Talent

The lifeblood of an MLM business lies in its network members. Hence, the recruitment and retention of talented individuals is central to the long-term success of your firm.

- Ideal Target: Understand who makes an ideal member for your network. Highlight the benefits your MLM opportunity can bring to them.

- Provide Training: Train your recruits in sales and product knowledge. Empower them with the right tools and knowledge.

- Retention: Connect with your network members on a personal level. Provide adequate mentorship and rewards to increase the sense of belonging and involvement.

# 11.5. Leveraging Technology

Harness the power of the latest technologies to gain a competitive edge and ensure sustainable profits in the long run. Your application of technology should aim to simplify processes, increase efficiency, and support your growth strategies.

- Automation Tools: Use automation tools for recurring tasks like email marketing, customer relationship management, and data analysis.

- Social Media: Utilise platforms like Facebook, Instagram, Twitter, and LinkedIn to connect with your potential recruits and customers, share content, and promote your products.

- Track Key Metrics: Use analytic tools to keep track of key performance indicators (KPIs). They help identify areas for improvement and measure success.

To wrap up, charting a course towards long-term prosperity in the MLM landscape demands more than just an entrepreneurial spirit. It calls for resilience, a learning mindset, clear goal setting, robust online presence, ace recruitment strategies, and a forward-thinking approach to embracing technology. Remember, success in MLM is a marathon, not a sprint. Print these strategies into your business DNA and let your persistent efforts propel your MLM venture to unparalleled heights.